DRIVEN

—— TO ——

SUCCEED

DRIVEN
— TO —
SUCCEED

Excel your personal growth to fuel your
career growth

SCOTT BIEHL

Scott Biehl
scott@driventosucceed.coach
driventosucceed.coach

Driven to Succeed, Scott Biehl—1st ed. 978-1-955242-90-5

PRAISE FOR SCOTT BIEHL

"I have known Scott Biehl for approximately 40 years, going back to when we worked at a restaurant together when we were young. We became friends, and eventually, we were office partners at Michael Automotive. When Scott was first hired, he worked 12 days and sold 15 cars. He was very proud of himself. I told him, "Talk to me in 30 days," which we still laugh about.

Within a year, Scott was recruited to go into Finance at a Honda Store. 5 years later, I left and went to work a new Honda Store that was opening. Scott had already applied, and we started working together. The owners told us their goal was to someday get to 100 cars per month. Scott and I looked at each other and smiled–we did it the 3rd month. I have hired, trained, and worked with more than 50 managers in my career, and here are a few things that stood out about Scott:

1) *At 21 years old, Scott had detailed, written goals for ages 25, 30, 35, and 40 years old–and he accomplished them all.*
2) *Scott's competitive nature would not allow him to accept 2nd place.*
3) *Scott was in a major car accident in which he broke his hip, and as soon as he was able to walk again, he started running with me. He said he was going to wear out, not rust out.*

4) *Our group played basketball every morning before work and started lifting weights daily.*

5) *Scott is an excellent trainer who takes the time to help people around him succeed. He still takes the time to teach me the ownership side of the car business.*

6) *Scott is a true friend you can count on at any time of crisis or accomplishment.*

7) *Silent but deadly, tenacious, resilient, aggressive, and a true friend. That's why I nicknamed him "Killer" 30+ years ago."*

–Gary Revis

"No quote can capture the individual Scott Biehl is. He is innovative, kind, full of love, and quite philanthropic. Scott only does well when there is a tangible and challenging goal ahead of him. Give him the goal to exercise for 75 straight days, and he will not only do it, but he will go above and beyond to exceed that goal and even include a bunch of people to do it with him. He is a leader at best. A relentless leader."

–Jennifer "JZ" Zerling, CEO of JZ Fitness,
Fitness and Age Management Expert

"Scott is one of those rare individuals who can cast a big vision and accomplish it!"

–Dan Herwaldt, Retired Automotive Dealer and Executive

"Scott Biehl's friendship and mentorship proved to be instrumental in my career in the car business. I spent 32 years brokering new car dealerships at National Business Brokers and had the opportunity to make my first investment as an owner at Mercedes-Benz of Fresno in 2018. Scott Biehl entered my life as a partner and truly became a mentor. His willingness to show me the business and teach me department by department over months and months proved invaluable in helping me get to where I am today. Today, I have the privilege of being a partner in four dealerships, and I am the approved dealer principal of three. I can't express enough gratitude to Scott for how he's helped me accomplish my goals."

–Brady Schmidt,
President,
National Business Brokers

"I've worked in the automobile industry for nearly three decades, and I found Scott to have a unique leadership style. Scott encapsulates his knowledge and expertise in a way that empowers teams to perform at high levels in promoting customer goodwill, employee satisfaction, and dealership profitability. This style and strategy made us the #1 Jaguar Land Rover dealership in the USA."

–Steve Brown, General Manager,
Jaguar Land Rover Los Angeles

"Scott Biehl is obviously a smart businessman, but one thing I noticed that sets him apart is an unrelenting work ethic. That, paired with an intelligent process, is a winning scenario!"

–Wayne Harlan, Owner/Founder,
Innovative Fitness & Rehab

"Scott is a servant leader who has a steady track record of equipping others for success in business, and more importantly, in life. It has been said that every counselor has a counselor, every doctor has a doctor, and every leader not only has followers but is being mentored by somebody else. Driven by his passion for excellence in every aspect of life… Scott practices in his life what he preaches to others."

–Brent Deffenbacher

"I have known Scott Biehl for the last 10 years, and he is a person with vast resources. His business-savvy mindset has resulted in extraordinary business operations and successful execution. I enjoy business conversations outside of our medical discussions because Scott's ability to articulate the non-obvious provides me with insight that remains unparalleled."

–Dr Juan Chavez, CEO of Optimal Medical Group

"How do you translate passion for what you do into passion for WHO you work with? Scott has that incredible skill -- making stakeholders feel immensely valued, turning a transaction into a true relationship. There's not a team in this country that wouldn't rally behind a Scott-led program."

–Jeff Schieferle Uhlenbrock, Senior Vice President & Head of Commercial Banking, Fortress Bank

"Scott recruited me into the automotive industry in 1998, and his mentoring and coaching made lasting impressions on my career path for over two decades. The perseverance and desire for ambition Scott instilled in me helped me propel my career to what I've achieved in growth."

–Banu Grewal, General Manager, Kearny Mesa Hyundai

"There were so many lessons I learned while working for Scott. The impact he had on me and my career will never be forgotten. From the day I started to the moment I left Mercedes-Benz of Fresno, I will always remember how Scott mentored me, coached me, and most importantly - challenged me to be the best version of myself I could be. When Scott and I worked on deals together, I would sometimes have a question on which direction he wanted me to go. Without a doubt, Scott would tell me, "You already know what to do." Even though there were times I felt I didn't, Scott empowered me to make my own decisions. Every decision I made, right or wrong - Scott stood behind it. He was teaching me

what it meant to be confident in myself for the decisions I was making. Without Scott's guidance and trust in me, I would have never completed NADA Academy, an education and experience that I will have for the entirety of my career. Scott believed in my abilities, empowered me to make decisions, and gave me the tools to act on them in just 4 short years."

–Spencer Paul, General Sales Manager,
Porsche-Audi of Fresno

"I have known Scott as a client and a mentor for over a decade. He is an incredibly dynamic, flexible, creative, and forward-thinking dealer operator."

–Saad Rehan MBA, AFIP, Regional Finance & Insurance
Producer, Zurich Direct Markets

"Scott has been an exemplary and visionary mentor who is selflessly dedicated to making myself and our team the best they can be. He remains an excellent leader, teacher, and most importantly, friend. Scott's passion for his work is just as strong as his dedication to his family and friends. Thank you, Scott, for being an amazing person. I have newly developed skills to explore bigger and more exciting challenges in my future because of our time together."

–John Hernandez, General Manager,
Mercedes Benz of Fresno

"I have known Scott for about 10 years. The thing that strikes me about Scott is that he always had a goal to achieve success, and he never took his eye off the ball. I had no doubt that he would achieve all of his goals. Scott has achieved his success through perseverance and dedication. This trait becomes contagious amongst his team and is why his team gives their all at their jobs. I have gotten to know not only Scott but many of his team members. Scott has a unique ability to be knowledgeable about every aspect of his business, without micromanaging any aspect of it. He has complete trust in his people to own the jobs they were hired to perform."

–Michael Martin, Founder and CEO of Audvisor

"I have known and worked with Scott for over 20 years and watched him grow from a General Sales Manager to Owner and CEO and eventually even become the #1 JLR dealer in the country. Scott's ability to not only create the vision for growth but to map out and execute the game plan with his team is what sets him apart. I would recommend Scott to anyone or any organization looking to take their personal and professional growth to the next level!"

–George Karolis, President, Presidio Group

"One of Scott's greatest traits is his ability to relate to all kinds of people. In a world where many leaders look only to mold people in their image, Scott finds ways to create consensus while respecting diversity of opinion. This is a bit of the "secret sauce" he can share."

–Tracey Matura, Former MBUSA Executive

"Scott taught me the importance of creating a winning culture in the dealership. His ability to work with people and build a successful team is second to none. In my 20-year automotive career, I have never met someone like Scott who is able to align different backgrounds, personalities, and thought processes into one vision. He has a way of leading you to identify the answer to your problem so that you grow as an employee rather than giving you the answers to the test."

–Adam "Big Mess" Messick, General Manager,
Lithia Ford Lincoln of Fresno

FOREWORD

What a blueprint for life!!! Scott has put in a simple format a way to order your life for success. Certainly, the definition of success is cloaked in a working career template but that is only a portion of the success available by following Scott's process. Your ability to develop personal success will surely be impacted by the principles and wisdom that Scott lays out for you. Scott and I started as partners in business which brought us together as friends through the years. Our ability to connect on a personal level has allowed us to learn from each other, which is why I am so excited for this next chapter of his life.

Through many years of working with people in all sorts of different environments and relationships, I have noticed that teachable people achieve more. They tend to grow more and accomplish more in all areas of life. If you are teachable or want to become teachable this roadmap from Scott will be a meaningful tool to soak up wise principles to drive your life. Scott's succinct principles are packed with a life rooted in learning. Scott's desire is to share his wisdom in a way that truly creates a path to success. It takes hard work but if you commit to the process, your success is virtually guaranteed.

I know in my life that the deepest joy in my business success has been and are the relationships that I have in my work life. Scott is a friend that I treasure and have deep admiration for his heart's desire to help others. The way he lives his life is truly a life that anyone would desire to replicate. Scott has laid out exactly that!!!! These principles are tried and true. All one needs to do is to look at Scott's life to see them. Anyone will benefit from their exposure to Scott personally or through the experience of reading his book. May your life be an adventuresome journey that starts here!!

Jerry Heuer

CONTENTS

INTRODUCTION

Are you driven to succeed?

If you opened this book, I'm willing to bet you are...

And I bet you're in the same position that I was in years ago: you're an employee in the automotive industry or any industry for that matter, you're hungry to grow in your career, and you have a vision of what you want your future to look like... But you have no idea how to get there.

You're in the car with a destination in mind, but you don't have a map. And with so many voices out there claiming to have the answer to career growth, you're not sure who to listen to or where to begin.

I remember what that felt like. Not long after I started in the industry, I developed a vision for myself–a big vision–to own a dealership. I had no idea how I would get there, but through years of focus, hard work, and life lessons earned through failure, I built a map to my destination. Not only did I achieve the goal of owning a dealership, I owned multiple. My last dealership, which I sold not long before writing this book was the #1 Jaguar Land Rover dealer in the U.S.

I share that, not to brag, but to give you confidence that what I'm about to share with you works. It worked for me, and it has worked with countless team members and colleagues that I have shared it with as they rose through the ranks of the industry.

Along my path to success, I learned the value of having a mentor—someone who has achieved what you want to achieve and who is committed to helping you grow. After rising to the top of the automotive industry, I decided to shift my focus to mentoring others who are driven to succeed.

I wrote this book to share what I've learned on my own journey and through mentoring and coaching others in the automotive industry to make their dreams a reality.

The #1 game-changing lesson I want to share is that career growth starts with personal growth. If you want to climb the ranks at your organization and reach new levels of career achievement, you'll get nowhere if you don't look within and improve yourself. Your journey to success doesn't pause when you leave your workplace—it's a 24/7, totally encompassing commitment to become the best version of yourself... And then become even better...

Let this book guide you through a personal transformation journey that will impact every area of your life and supercharge your ability to win the career success you've been dreaming of.

But I warn you... Once you commit to personal growth, it will be hard for you to stop. When you accomplish your goal, you'll set an even bigger one...and then an even bigger one... You'll never be able to settle for mediocrity again, and you'll see each day as a challenge to push yourself a little farther and accomplish more than you did yesterday.

Meanwhile, as a byproduct of your commitment to growth, you'll get promoted more quickly, make more money, build connections with other high achievers, get healthier, feel happier, become more confident, become a positive influence on your loved ones, and achieve things you'd previously only dreamed of achieving. When you walk into a room, people will instantly be able to tell that you're driven to succeed because you'll radiate confidence, strength, and determination. You'll join the ranks of those who have let go of their fears and made their biggest dreams, their wildest ambitions, a reality.

I believe that anyone, with the right mindset, habits, and actions, can accomplish their goals, yet so many people choose to remain stagnant. They let their dreams remain "what-ifs," and life passes them by and leaves them with regrets. These people are afraid of the challenge and discomfort of personal growth, and as a result, they miss out on the dream life that could have been theirs. When others land their dream positions or when they watch their peers outperform them, they think, "Life isn't fair... That should be me!"

Yet the secret to success was within them all along...

You have two roads ahead of you. You can put down this book and stay where you are. You can let fear win and remain in your comfort zone, letting your dreams be nothing more than "what-ifs." Or you can take the leap and commit to personal growth. You can push past the fear and discomfort, knowing that your effort will someday pay off when you achieve your goals. You can unlock your full potential and discover the power of getting a little bit better each day.

What will you choose?

If you choose to commit to personal growth, I'm here to be your guide—as someone who has gone through this journey myself and coached others through their transformations.

In the rest of this book, I'll share the path to personal and career growth for those in the automotive industry who are driven to succeed.

CHAPTER 1

Making the Commitment

Why are you here?

Whether you're starting out in your career or in a position of leadership, what's motivating you to read this book?

If you're an employee at an organization, do you want to get promoted to a higher position? Do you want to make more money so you can improve your life? Do you feel stuck in your current position, and you're unsure how to move forward? Do you have big dreams of becoming a department head, general manager, or owner someday but have no idea how to make that happen?

If you're an organization leader—a general manager, a CEO, or an owner—why are you reading this book?

Are you looking for new ideas to grow your career or business? Are you struggling to build a cohesive team? Are you looking for a new approach to coach and motivate your team so you can elevate your success?

If you're searching for a way to increase your profits, the answer lies in your people. When your team is committed to growth, they'll create a better experience for your customers. When your customers are thrilled with your organization, sales and referrals are attracted to you like a magnet. There's no sales trick or "overnight success" strategy that will bring you more long-term profit than building a world-class team.

But how do you begin to elevate your team and set your organization on the path to winning big?

In this book, I'll share a transformational process that will allow everyone on your team to "level up"...and level up again...and again...and again...

This process begins a snowball effect that brings more profit & happier customers to the organization, gives people the tools to climb through the ranks and achieve their dream careers, and sets each individual on the path to a more fulfilling life, with the power to accomplish any goal they want to and control their destinies. Everyone wins...and keeps winning.

But before we launch into this journey, let's take a moment to get clarity on why you're here.

If you're an employee, you picked up this book because you want something to change. Wherever you are in your career, you wish you were further along...But you feel stuck, and you're not sure how to push forward and reach your goal.

What roadblocks are you experiencing? What stands in the way of you getting to the next level in your career?

Some people face mental roadblocks. They think, "I'm not good enough... I'll never be a general manager... Why should I waste my time trying?" or "If I get promoted to sales manager, my friends on the sales team won't like me... I should just stay where I am" or " The last three managers in this position got fired. What if I move up and then I am the fourth to be fired?"

Others feel that they face roadblocks in their organization. They believe they aren't getting the attention and training they'd like from their boss, so they don't see how they'll reach the next level without the support of their leaders. When it comes time for promotions, they feel constantly overlooked and wish the boss would take notice. This can be a frustrating feeling...

To overcome it, you need to consider the problem from your boss's perspective. Leaders are under a tremendous amount of pressure, and their time is limited. If you're not proactively seeking out guidance from them, they may be so swamped by their own responsibilities that they don't think to check in about your career goals. And if you feel you're constantly being overlooked for promotions, the truth may be that you aren't setting yourself apart as a standout player on the team. That can be a hard reality to accept, but once you accept it, you can take productive steps to become that "star player" so your boss has no choice but to take notice.

> "My friend Scott would often say... Success is not solely determined by talent; it is a combination of various factors and attitudes."
>
> —Manuel Prieto, President, Prieto Automotive Company

Once you identify your current roadblocks, ask yourself, "Are these roadblocks valid, or are they just excuses?"

People often use mental roadblocks as excuses to stay in their comfort zone. When people think, "I can't do this," "They're never going to promote me," or "I'm just not an early morning person," what they're really saying is, "I'm scared of change, so to protect myself from failure and discomfort, I'm going to stay right where I am."

But if you've picked up this book, you're no longer content with "right where you are." You want to change.

The first step to change is acknowledging the excuses you tell yourself and letting them go. We need to unlock your mindset so you can believe that change is possible.

If you've been telling yourself, "I'm not good enough," realize that ANYONE can be good enough—if they put in the work to be.

If you've been telling yourself, "They'll never promote me," recognize that you haven't yet put in the effort to become a no-brainer candidate for promotion. Leaders only promote people who they can see are ready for a promotion. Drop your excuse, put in the work, and see what happens.

So...should you even read this book?

Before you read the rest of this book, I want you to commit to change. If you don't, reading this book may end up being a waste of your time. Real change that lasts and continues to grow starts with YOU!

Often, a person's actions don't match their desires. If someone tells me, "I want to be the CEO someday," but they go out and party every night after work, hit the snooze button six times, and never participate in meetings, their actions don't match their desires. They have a fantasy, not a goal.

If your actions don't match your desires, you haven't yet committed to change. In this book, we are going to take those desires and help you create the habits that will propel you to make lasting changes when you commit to them.

Are you ready to commit?

Once you make the commitment, you need to follow through with it. If you commit, keep it for a few days, and then give up, your chances of going back and recommitting again are slim. You'll cling even tighter to your comfort zone.

To prevent that from happening, you need to prepare yourself for commitment.

Remind yourself of why you want to change your life. What is your ultimate goal? What do you want the future to look like? Accept that this future can be yours if you commit to growth.

It's also helpful to get buy-in from the people around you. If your friends and family know you're pursuing success, they can support you and motivate you to keep going. Sometimes, just knowing that your friends and family are aware of the goal you're pursuing makes you want to keep pushing on... You don't want to let them down or be embarrassed if you give up.

If you're married or have a significant other, you may want to have your partner read this book, too, so they can understand what you're trying to accomplish and hold you accountable to the commitment you've made. A transformation like this isn't just about you... When you achieve more career success, you'll make more money and be able to give your family a better life. Remember that your spouse and kids are rooting for you to succeed so your whole family can have a brighter future. I am pretty certain that when you entered into this career, you did not go around telling everyone you wanted to be "average" at it... You wanted to be the BEST at it!

You may want to share your game plan for personal and professional growth with your boss or coworkers. Mentioning to a boss or mentor that you're taking steps toward personal growth shows initiative. And if you have a buddy in the same position as you who is also looking to make a change, you can work together through this process and motivate each other to keep going. Sometimes, this can be infectious, and one or two team members can inspire a whole organization to commit to this transformation.

Now that you've committed, let's begin the journey…

CHAPTER 2

Overcoming Fear

Why are we talking about fear in a book about the car business?

Fear is the #1 factor that holds people back from achieving their goals.

If you're committed to growth, the first step is to overcome fear. Most people won't admit to fear, but we all deal with it. If you don't let go of fear, you'll sabotage your progress.

There are two major types: the fear of failure and the fear of success.

People often self-sabotage out of a fear of failure. For example, if someone has the opportunity to pursue a promotion, he or she may be afraid that he won't get it and will hold himself back from pursuing it. Rejection and failure can sting, so it's easier and more comfortable to sit back and not try rather than putting ourselves out there.

But many people also suffer from the fear of success. A person may hold himself back from pursuing a promotion because he's afraid that he'll get the position and leave behind the life he's used to.

Both the fear of failure and the fear of success boil down to a fear of leaving your comfort zone. It's much easier to play it safe and stick with what you know.

At an organization, sticking to your comfort zone often means being afraid to step out of the "herd." If you're a salesperson, you may have hung out with the other salespeople for years. What will happen when you get promoted and now you're their boss? Will they dislike you because you moved to a higher rank? Will they respect you as a leader? Will you lose friendships with coworkers you enjoy spending time with? These fears hold many people back from climbing the ladder at an organization, but they aren't productive. Do you really want to let a fear of what others will think hold you back from the life of your dreams?

To let go of your fears, it helps to remember that you aren't just doing this for yourself. You're doing it for your family. The time you spend at work takes away valuable family time. Maximize the value of that time by growing your career and your income to give your family a better life.

Fear is often selfish. It gives us excuses to not perform at our best when others are depending on us. What lengths will you go to to give your kids a nicer house, exciting vacations, and better education? Are you going to let fear stop you from transforming your family's life?

A Winner's Mentality

If you're going to grow, you need to shift to a winner's mentality.

Rather than fearing loss, know that you're going to win.

"Winning" doesn't mean you never make mistakes or experience failure. Growth is winning. If you're better today than you were yesterday, you're a winner.

External wins aren't the only type of wins. You may find that a winner's mindset correlates to having more external wins, but these are merely a byproduct of a winner's mindset. It doesn't matter if you're chosen for the seat on the board or not—ultimately, that decision is in someone else's hands, and you have no control over it besides showing up as your best self. So rather than staking our "wins" only on external rewards, we're going to focus on growth.

Growth = Winning

When you understand that growth = winning, every failure and mistake becomes a helpful, productive step on your path to ultimate, big-picture success. When your coworker is chosen for the promotion over you, that's not a failure—it's a growth opportunity to assess what this person does better than you and learn from them. Maybe you get the promotion next year, but either way, you've won because you've improved yourself. I watched people get promoted in front of me in my career, but it only pushed me to work harder to get to the next stage. In the end, I got promoted four or five positions above these people because they stopped growing while I continued to grow.

When you put in the work, you end up better than you were, and that's a win for you. That can be measurable even during times when the outward win isn't there yet. The outward might be the promotion you're working towards. You don't necessarily have final control over that—someone else makes the decision, though you should give them every reason possible to choose you first. But even if you aren't chosen for an outward win, you can win by executing habits daily that move you towards your goal. Each day, you win by making incremental improvements. Whether it's increasing how much you can lift at the gym or studying a new sales strategy, these daily improvements are wins.

These daily wins lead to big wins over time, but you may not see the big wins right away. That's why it's key to appreciate the small, daily wins and focus on getting better each day. If you're focused only on the big wins, you may get discouraged when you don't see them immediately.

> When I worked with Scott, it wasn't about getting a big win. It was about getting 1% better each day. Scott helped me learn to focus on the 1%, and when I did that, I would look back and see all of the wins I was able to accomplish by getting 1% better each day.
>
> –Spencer, my mentee

You can keep winning even when it looks like you're stuck. I once spent ten years as a sales manager at a dealership… I had offers to leave and take a higher-level position at a different organization, but even though I wasn't moving up, I was winning because I was learning from my bosses, who were mentors to me. I didn't want to give up that daily growth and learning. Because of my accumulated daily growth, I eventually took an offer with another organization as a general sales manager, and within six months, I was promoted from general sales manager to general manager of that dealership. It looked like an overnight success, but it was due to those ten years I spent "winning" by learning and growing each day. To take it a step further, eight years later, I put a partnership together and purchased the Mercedes-Benz dealership I was working at. I went from a sales manager in a Honda store to an owner of a Mercedes dealership within 8 years. If you feel like you're "stuck" in a position, take advantage of that position to learn everything you can and be the best at that position…And trust that your growth will eventually pay off as long as you keep getting better each day.

If you're getting up every day, giving it your all, and concentrating on growth, you're winning. It doesn't matter what the score is.

It's like a football game where one team takes twelve minutes to get to the end zone and score a touchdown, and then the other team scores a touchdown in thirty seconds. Both teams scored the same amount of points—it doesn't matter that it took them different amounts of time to get there.

My journey of spending ten years as a sales manager and then quickly advancing to general manager is like a quarterback running the ball for a long time and then suddenly making a few quick passing plays that take him to a touchdown. To be able to execute this play, the quarterback had to spend years waking up early each day to go to practice and focus on improving. Not only that, he had to spend time in the "off season" preparing himself to be the starter and not just make the team. We don't see this part of the journey... We just see the exciting touchdown that makes the whole stadium stand up and cheer.

Sometimes, you need to be in the trenches grinding for a while and trusting that, if you're growing day by day, your work will someday pay off.

Sometimes the whole team can feel stuck. The work they're doing is decent, but they're not living up to their full potential of performing at the level the CEO wants. At this stage, moving toward success requires the team to shift towards a winner's mentality and keep making changes until an "overnight success" happens. At that point, the team needs to focus on the goal of TODAY and then execute that tomorrow and the next day and the next day... Which then turns into days, weeks, and months of success.

Growth is like chipping away at a brick wall until it crumbles down. Little by little, you'll make progress, but it's key to not become frustrated when success doesn't come right away.

What do you have to lose?

If you accept that the key to success is shifting to a winner's mentality, the rest of this book will give you the roadmap for living as a winner.

CHAPTER 3

Growth

Growth doesn't start at work. Growth starts with you.

Do you want to change? Are you ready for the change? As you're recognized for your positive change, are you ready for the reaction? Does this scare you or excite you? Or a little of both?

How much time are you applying to your personal growth goals versus your work goals?

Too many people rely on work to help them grow when what will help you achieve your professional goals is doing things outside of work to grow personally.

It's not up to your boss or manager to help you grow and advance to the next level. You need to put in time outside of work to change your habits. Avoid excuses like, "Well, my boss never gave me sales training, so I'm not good at sales." Instead, realize that it's up to you. If you want to be better at sales, build your own curriculum and study sales outside of work.

Personal growth looks different for everyone. We each have strengths and weaknesses. Someone who's already fit may not need to focus on building a habit of going to the gym—that already comes easily to him or her. His or her area for growth may be building a habit of reading books. It's all about balance.

The two most common areas of personal growth to start with are mindset and fitness.

Mindset is how you think. What inputs are you putting into your brain? Are you taking in positive or negative information? How does the way you think affect the actions you take? Do your actions align with your goals?

Physical fitness keeps your body and mind energized and healthy. But more than that, tackling physical fitness goals teaches you discipline. It trains your mind to stick to a routine and endure short-term discomfort for the sake of long-term growth. If you want to succeed in the workplace, you'll need discipline in spades, and physical fitness is a great way to harness this skill.

> "The mornings I wake up at four in the morning and get my butt to the gym, I just feel like I'm in such a better headspace. When I walk in the door, I feel like I can take on the world. It feels like I'm in that scene in *The Matrix*—time slows down and the bullets are whizzing past me, and I can take on anything because I'm operating at a different speed. I don't have a pit in my stomach thinking, "What could go wrong?" Instead, I think, "Hey, what can I accomplish

today?" And I know that 90% of the people I'm competing against don't do that, so it puts me a leg above the rest."

–Adam, my mentee

"Physical exercise brings mental clarity. When I was working on the 75 Hard challenge, I had never been more confident showing up to work. I'd wake up at 5:30 to get a workout in, and then I'd show up to work and everyone else was rubbing the sleep out of their eyes because they just woke up, rolled out of bed, and came to work. I'd look around the room and think, "That's my competition. Those are the people I have to beat out for the next role." I started to develop a confidence that was infectious."

–Spencer, my mentee

When you've grown in these two areas, you can leverage your growth at work and watch the magic happen.

Are you trending up in your personal growth? No matter which area you're focused on improving, each day you should be getting better little by little. The growth between one day and the next may be minimal, but as long as it's trending up, you're on the right track. Over time, you'll be able to look back and see how far you've come.

Developing Your Goals

To begin your growth journey, we'll establish your 5-year goal, your 3-year goal, your 1-year goal, and your monthly goal.

Where do you want to be in 5 years? Take a moment to visualize what your life looks like.

Your 3-year goal is when all of the habits you begin today pay off and show results. What will your life look like if you accomplish your goals of working out every day and reading two books a month? How will these habits propel you toward your 5-year goal? By committing to your habits for three years, you'll achieve a greater degree of consistency and self-discipline that will serve you not only in your career but also personally for the rest of your life.

What skills and habits do you need to develop this year that will bring you closer to your 5-year goal? Visualize what your life is like after committing to these habits for the next twelve months. What do you look like physically? What do you feel like mentally? What people are you surrounded by? What recognitions have you earned at work?

Each month of the year, you'll set monthly goals for your daily and weekly habits. At the end of the month, you'll measure your progress and alter your goals for the next month so you keep improving.

Each month, you set the bar higher while also making adjustments to monthly goals that aren't working so you can stay on track with your big-picture goals. Your monthly goals carry you to your yearly goals and, eventually, to your five-year goal.

When I was in my twenties, I broke my hip in three places in a car accident and had three screws put in my hip. I decided that I didn't want this injury to hold me back, so I began setting fitness goals to push myself. I ran half marathons, did triathlons, and cycled 50,000 miles in ten years. Beyond pushing myself physically, these goals built my mental fortitude.

Most people set goals in this way, "My goal is to make $__ in sales this month, so let's divide that number by four and see how much in sales I need to make in a week." That's result-based. Simply knowing how much you want to make in sales won't get you any closer to making it. But if you think, "What are the five things I need to do every day that will help me reach my goal?", these habits will create the condition for the result. Focus on executing habits that, when executed, will achieve the desired results.

The plan always changes... the goal does not change. This is why we focus on monthly goals. If your five-year goal shifts due to a life event or a big epiphany, it's easy to change your monthly goals to meet the changing landscape of your life.

Progress isn't always steady. For example, if your goal is to make a certain amount of sales in a year, that number may not look the same every month due to patterns in people's spending habits (for example, January tends to be a slow month for buying cars. This is why we focus on goals that are action-based, not result-based. Adapt yourself month to month so you can achieve your year-end goals rather than assuming every month will look the same. When I was leading my dealerships, I used January and February to focus on training. It was slower, so we had more time to focus on learning and preparing for the months ahead.

Self-Accountability

You're the conductor of your growth. No one is making it happen for you. If you want to see your goals become reality, you need to learn self-accountability.

Journaling is a way of achieving self-accountability. You're looking at yourself in the mirror every day and saying, "Did I do the things I set out to do? Did I do my non-negotiables or did I negotiate with myself to do something that took me off the path of where I wanted to go?"

If you did wander off the path, don't get discouraged and throw the entire plan away. Things happen, and not hitting your goals for one day won't sabotage your long-term plan. Use the days you get off track as learning experiences to figure out what you need to change to make it more likely that you won't miss a day again. And if you miss a day, get back on track the very next day. It's easy to get discouraged and turn one missed day into several. And the more days you miss, the easier it is to come up with excuses to miss another.

When I was training for a triathlon, the coaches would tell us, "If you need to miss a day once in a while because your body isn't cooperating, that's fine. Missing two days is not advisable. But if you miss three days, you're toast." After three days, you would get comfortable again and think, "Why would I want to wake up at 5 in the morning and swim in cold water? I'll just stay here under my warm covers." Soon, that can spiral into, "Eh, I don't need to compete in the race anyway. It's out of town and it'll be a hassle to get there. Maybe next year." Then, when all your buddies compete in the triathlon and tell you how amazing it was, you feel regret. You'll feel this same regret in business if you get off track with your goals and see others get promoted to positions you aspire to. You'll think, "Man, that could've been me. I was set to get promoted, too, if I had only stayed on track."

Progress is made through consistency. Consistency isn't sexy, but it is the key. It feels boring sometimes, but the boring leads to the exciting. Boring is part of the process of success. The monotony of doing the same thing over and over again each day to stay on track can tempt you to give up... But what's not boring is making millions, helping others grow by being philanthropic, riding in private jets, being recognized as the #1 dealer in the country for your brand, and taking incredible vacations... Keep your eyes on the prize.

The boring part never stops. But you can make what was once boring fun and exciting by creating a game around your habits. The best way to do this is through friendly competition. If you and a few friends are pursuing the same goal, you can challenge each other and hold each other accountable. I felt the best way to get this going at work was to do something personally to push me out of my comfort zone. I would sign up for races, half marathons, and cycling events of 100 miles in a day. Then, I would train as hard as I could every morning before work for those events. This would not only train my body for the next race but also train my mind to do the daily habits that were boring but necessary at work. The harder I pushed myself physically each day, the better I became at work. My best training days at 5 am were my hardest days, and those became my easiest days at work. When you train for two hours in the morning at high intensity, everything else seems easy in comparison after that.

The minute you start seeing results come in, it all clicks… But you have to push through that initial period of grinding and doing the work before you begin to see the result, and that's where most people fail.

Boring turns the pilot light on. Once you get past boring and you start to see success, the fire starts to burn. Once the furnace is on and it's hot, there's no stopping you. You cannot turn that furnace down. If you keep going down that path, you will get to where you want to go. There's nobody that can stop you. Not your boss, not the economy, nobody. Once that is lit and the flame gets turned up, it's powerful.

Developing your comprehensive growth plan

Each month, you'll write down a "growth plan" of your goals. What will you do this month to get closer to your five-year goal?

I like to break monthly goals into four areas:

Motivation/commitment—Are you motivated and committed to get where you want to go?

Skills—What skills do you need to learn to achieve your goals? What's your plan for learning these skills?

Action—How will you turn what you've learned into a habit?

Health & Fitness—Have you built the foundation for success in your mind and body?

These four areas should be in balance. No one area should overpower the others.

I love motivational books, but they can be dangerous. If you only read motivational books and never read actionable books, your motivation won't take you anywhere. You'll feel pumped up when you get out of bed in the morning, but if you don't combine that with action toward your goals, your motivation will remain only a feeling. Balance consuming motivational material with material that teaches you actionable steps to build habits and disciplines. Without taking action, motivation may make you feel great, but it will keep you stuck where you are.

For all of your monthly goals, how will you measure your progress? For example, if you want to run in the mornings, will you track this goal by minutes or by distance? If you want to read more, will you keep track of the pages you read in a day or the books you read in a month?

Once you have your growth plan, each day, spend five to ten minutes every night before bed journaling. Write down what progress you made that day and how you felt about it. If you're not on track, figure out how you can get back on track tomorrow and then add those actionable items to your daily task list for the next day.

Your growth plan has to be in service of your goal. If you don't have a goal, you may be doing things without a clear purpose, and this unfocused approach can keep you stuck.

But if your growth plan is aligned with your goals, slowly but surely, you'll get where you want to go.

CHAPTER 4

Visualizing Success

What does "being successful" mean to you?

Success means something different for everyone. Before you can pursue your version of success, you need to get clear on what it looks like.

Some people measure success by money. Their goal is to make a certain amount of money per year so they can have the financial freedom to pursue the life they want to live.

Others may aspire to have freedom of time. They may consider themselves successful when they reach a leadership position that allows them to control their own schedules rather than having a boss set their schedule.

For many, success is measured by experiences. They want to look back on what they've achieved with a sense of pride. The experience could look like being honored with an award for your work at the organization or being able to take your family on a dream vacation.

Some measure success by what they're able to do for their family. They may dream of the day they're successful enough to send their kids to a top college, buy a home to make memories in, or afford to let their spouse leave the workforce to raise the kids.

Others feel they'll only be successful when they reach a certain role or job title. But I believe success isn't defined by reaching a certain role. Being the very best you can be in your current role makes you successful. The best sales manager at one store might be more successful than a mediocre dealer at another store.

When I was in the sales manager position for 10 years, rather than feeling like I wasn't successful because I wasn't in a higher position, I decided to become successful at being a sales manager. I wanted our store to outsell the other stores in the region and score higher than them on the customer satisfaction index. I monitored the key point indicators each month and outlined my plan to achieve our goals. Later, when I was interviewing for higher positions, I was a better candidate because I had demonstrated I could be successful as a sales manager and had approached that role as if I were a general sales manager. If you're a sales manager, be the best sales manager there is and keep track of all of the things you're doing so that when you get to the next level, you're prepared.

Visualizing Recognition

Now that you know what your definition of success is, visualize being recognized for your achievements—inside your organization, at the corporate level, or in the industry.

What would it mean to you to be recognized as #1? The best sales manager at your store? The top performer in sales in your market? To have an article written about you in automotive news?

What does that look like when you go home and share the news with your family? What does it look like when your peers call to congratulate you? What does it look like when your boss shakes your hand and thanks you for your work?

What does that feel like? When you've felt that feeling of achievement once, you'll want to feel it over and over again.

When you visualize that recognition, you're already feeling rewarded for it. Visualizing recognition helps you have the motivation to do the often boring and hard work of pursuing your goals.

Winners not only visualize success, they manifest it!

Manifest the life and career you want, and work towards it every single day. You are the only one that is in control of your success.

"When you visualize your success, you can see that everything you want is out there waiting for you, like a reward—you just have to put in the work to get it.

> When I started working in the car business, I wrote down my goal: 'I'm going to be a general manager before I'm 30 years old.' I accomplished that goal, and now I'm working toward bigger and better goals... It's so important to visualize your goals because it gives you something to chase for. If we're going to work 12-15 hours a day, are we doing it just to grow our bank accounts, or are we doing it for something bigger? Monetary rewards are cool, but to me, self-growth is the most important reward."
>
> –Spencer, my mentee

Tom Brady, Michael Jordan, Tiger Woods, and Michael Phelps all visualized success long before they reached the top. They all had challenges and setbacks, but they all overcame the fear of losing and adopted a winner's mentality.

I visualized being the number one dealer in the country while negotiating the deal to buy Jaguar Land Rover Los Angeles. In my mind, we were already number one. I just had to put in the work and assemble a team that had the winning mentality to be number one. I knew when I bought it that I didn't just want to focus on making money for the store. I wanted to focus on doing everything required to be number one. We talked about it with the staff every single day in every meeting. At the end of each month, we would get a ranking report, and if we were ranked 10th in the nation, I would tell the staff, "We are the number one store in the nation. This ranking report doesn't show it, but look at the growth we've already had. Look at the processes we're putting in place. We're gearing up to be number one." I would say, "How many used cars a month could you sell if you had zero roadblocks?" At the time, we were selling about 80 used cars a month. The staff would say, "I think we could sell 100. Maybe 110." I would say, "How many does the Carmax down the street sell?" "500 a month." I would say, "Why is our goal only 100?" The staff said, "Well, Carmax has marketing. They have a bigger inventory." I would say, "I told you I would take all the obstacles away from you. What if I bought us the lot across the street, bought us 1,000 used cars, spent $200,000 a month on marketing, and hired 30 people to sell those cars? Could we sell 500 a month?" Everyone said, "Of course we could." I'd say, "Exactly. That's my point. You're not visualizing big enough what we could do if we take all of our obstacles out of the way. Now that we know what obstacles we need to remove, we can work on removing them."

We talked about and visualized the recognition we would all receive for being #1—and sure enough, 14 months later, we were the #1 Jaguar Land Rover dealership in the USA, and the money followed. Not only were we #1 in sales, but we were highly profitable as well.

If you're at the salesperson level and there's a ranking board, look at how many cars the number one salesperson has sold. Visualize how many cars you'd have to sell to beat that salesperson. Then, you can put a plan together of what it would take to make that happen. Executing this plan will take work, but visualizing your success first is a crucial step.

Focus on your vision for success, and nothing will stop you from making it a reality.

When I was a young sales manager in my 20s, I would sit with my co-worker and fellow manager, also in his 20s, and we would talk about what it would be like to be a GM and then owner someday. We would visualize what it would look like to own and run our own dealership group. We spoke about our goals and the work it would take to achieve them. We pushed each other to get better every day. He would push me to read more books and learn as much as I could. We would meet at 5 am for a long run or to cycle for 40-50 miles, always pushing each other to get faster and go longer. We did the same at work. Our families became close, our kids grew up together, and we wanted the best for each other even though we were competing for the same positions as we moved up.

Sitting there daily and visualizing what we could accomplish in our careers propelled us both to incredible success. Neither one of us came from money, and both of us had only a high school diploma, but we never stopped believing in what we could accomplish.

I became the owner and CEO of a few dealerships, and in that journey, I took a struggling dealership to the #1 Jaguar Land Rover Dealership in the USA. My co-worker now owns an automotive group that consists of 7 franchises in three different cities. We still talk and visualize together to this day and share our goals and aspirations. We know that what we visualized and manifested these past 30 years has become a reality for both of us. This visualization, along with the consistency of our daily habits, took us to the top, and I know others can have the same success using the same tools as we have done and continue to do.

CHAPTER 5

Self Discipline - The Road to Success

When we're children, our parents monitor our habits: what we eat, what time we go to bed, what we wear, and if we finish our homework. When you become an adult, you're left to monitor your own habits. That takes self-discipline. In adulthood, monitoring our habits is difficult because we have the freedom to make our own choices. We have the freedom to buy a dozen donuts and eat them in one sitting if we want to, but is that the best decision? When you were ten years old, a parent or grandparent would be there to tell you why that's not a good decision, but now, it's up to you to make decisions that will lead you to long-term success rather than choosing only what is easy, fun, and comfortable. If you're a parent, it's to tell your kids, "Do this, but don't do that." When we become adults, why don't we do it for ourselves?

We're supposed to grow up and take on these disciplinary responsibilities from our parents, but many people don't.

We have to become self-disciplined.

Our habits, good and bad, dictate who we are and how we are perceived by others. The better we are at regulating ourselves from our bad habits and replacing them with good habits, the better we will become in our personal growth and career growth.

When you start to discipline yourself, your confidence increases. You have a better self-image because you know you're transforming and creating better habits. When you walk into a room, people see you differently because they can see and feel your confidence. You're walking with purpose because you have goals, a vision, and a task list. You're no longer following the herd mentality and you begin to become a leader. A chain reaction starts to occur... When you start to change, your vibration goes up.

Have you ever walked into a business and, without knowing anyone or looking at a name tag, spotted the leader right from the get-go? Why is that? It's the "vibe" or vibration that you are picking up from them. It's the way they walk, talk, and carry themselves, and how others react when they walk by. That confidence is due to the self-discipline they use to get better every day.

Personal Growth Precedes Career Growth

If you want to grow in your career, what you do outside of work is equally as important as what you do inside of work. You need to improve yourself before the results show outwardly in your career. Some readers may be tempted to pursue only career growth and skip the personal habits discussed in this chapter, but it's difficult to have career growth without building the foundation of self-discipline through these habits.

What habits have the biggest impact?

1. Set a routine

How do you spend your time? We all get the same 24 hours in a day, but how you spend those hours is up to you. Setting a routine helps you take control of your time rather than moving through your day with no focus or purpose.

Set a routine with the time you wake up and the time you go to sleep. Then, you can make a plan to maximize the hours left in a day with work, exercise, family time, reading, and rejuvenating your mind and body.

Make a list each night of what you want to achieve the next day and what time slots you'll perform each task during. This list should align with your monthly goals, both personal and professional. If they don't, when you reach the end of the month, you'll make excuses for why you didn't reach your monthly goals.

It's important to put your goals and routine on paper. (Or on your phone—in our digital era, countless goal-setting apps allow you to track your progress). How you write it down doesn't matter, as long as your method works for you.

When establishing new habits, you have to execute the habit every day for thirty days straight to establish it as a routine. If you fall off for one day, your 30 days start over the next day.

Life's distractions can derail you from your goals. Every day, something out of your control could happen. A family member gets sick. Your boss gets fired. Your car breaks down. The key to establishing self-discipline is to practice your habits even when unexpected inconveniences pop up. Stop looking for an out and start looking for an in! Most people are looking for a way out of something. Bad weather to cancel a run outside, high interest rates to negate a big purchase like a house or a dealership. A reason or an "out" to NOT start new daily habits.

Do this over a few months, a few years, ten years, or even decades, and see where you end up. I promise you it won't be where you need to be. So instead of looking for an "out," start looking for an "in"--a place to jump in and start the process of daily transformation to change your life and career path forever. An "in" will transform your life, but your so-called "easy outs" will haunt you forever.

> "Keeping our daily habits is what keeps us grounded."
>
> –Spencer, my mentee

Setting a routine is a keystone habit—it sets the foundation for getting the other habits done. If you're not intentional with your time, it'll be nearly impossible to make progress toward your goals.

One of the key habits that has always helped me stay on track to work out in the mornings is that I set out my workout clothes the night before. If I am going to run, I check the weather the night before and place my running shoes, socks, shorts, gloves, hat, water bottle, etc. beside my bed. I have done this religiously as a habit for almost 40 years. I do not want any variables in my routine that could distract me from my goal of working out that day. Once these types of habits start in your life, you will adopt similar ones in your professional life. This will instill good discipline and habits to stay on track in everything you do.

2. Health & Fitness

When I bring up health and fitness goals, many people think I mean that you need to build six-pack abs or win a marathon. The point of health and fitness goals isn't to chase results such as losing weight or becoming an elite athlete. It's to build discipline, take care of your body, and gain control of your health.

If I know I'm going to have a hard day at work, I plan to do a workout that morning that's even harder. I want to make sure my workout is the hardest part of my day. No matter what is on my daily task list, I can look forward to it because I know it'll be easier than the workout I've already accomplished. Doing this builds my grit and stamina for the day to come.

You need energy and stamina to be able to put in the effort necessary to succeed at your job. Getting your blood flowing in the morning is important for your energy and mental clarity. Most importantly—building healthy habits makes you feel amazing.

At my dealership, I consciously created a culture where the team was motivated to work together toward their health and fitness goals. They would use FitBits to remind them to take a five-minute walk around the dealership if they had been stuck sitting at a desk for an hour. Groups would often walk together to get lunch. I paid for a yoga teacher to come in the evenings twice a week so anyone who wanted to could take a free class after work. We also organized a 5K walk for an Alzheimer's charity and encouraged employees to participate.

If you're a leader, implementing activities like this can build team morale at your organization while also helping people realize the power of cultivating self-discipline through health and fitness.

3. Appearance

When I say "appearance," I don't mean you need to look like you're on the cover of a magazine or become focused on vanity. But cultivating a professional, polished appearance sets the tone for how others see you and how you see yourself.

When you look at yourself in the mirror before you go to work and see yourself looking put-together, it boosts your confidence. And when others see you come into work looking like you're ready to hit the ground running, it makes a positive impression.

Cultivating a put-together, motivated appearance is often one of the ways people notice the transformation you're undergoing. Others who are scared and fearful to make their own transformations may start asking you how you're doing it. All of a sudden, you start to become a leader. You start to influence others to start their own transformations, and the culture of the company improves because the whole team is committed to growth. When the culture changes, the store enjoys more success and makes more money for everyone.

Many people are frustrated because their bosses don't give them recognition. Improving your appearance to reflect your personal growth is an easy way to get others to notice that you're making changes in your life. When your bosses see that all of a sudden, you're showing up early and dressed sharply, they'll notice that you're working toward personal and career growth and be more likely to mentor you or help you move toward the next level.

Transforming your appearance doesn't necessarily mean you need to walk into work wearing a tuxedo. Each store has its own company culture that may reflect the brand, region, or clientele. What you wear may differ depending on what the expectations are at your particular store, but whatever it is, you need to wear the best and most polished version of that. Iron your shirt instead of wearing a wrinkled one. Wear clean, shined shoes rather than scuffed ones. These details may seem small, but they signal that you're a disciplined and responsible person.

If you want a higher position in the company, dress like you're already in that position. The leaders in the company will find it easier to see you in that position if you do. If the salespeople typically wear polo shirts, but the general manager wears a suit and tie, wear a suit and tie. The first day, your peers might say, "Why are you wearing a suit and tie?" But if you start dressing like that every day, you'll start getting higher results because your confidence is up. When a position opens up for a bigger role, your superiors will often be more likely to consider you for that role, simply because you look the part. Yes, you need the skills and performance to go with the new role, but all other things being equal, how you present yourself gives you an edge.

4. Preparation

When going into a meeting or presentation, do your homework early so that you are prepared for success. Don't get caught off-guard.

No matter if you're the presenter or listener, I want you to be prepared. If you're the one listening to the meeting, do you walk in prepared to focus and be alert? Do you have a pen and paper with you to take notes? Are you ready to ask thoughtful questions?

If you're a presenter, keep in mind that you're asking people to take time away from their day to have this meeting. Make sure you give a presentation that's worth their time and effectively communicates the information you need to deliver. Do you want to deliver something that's mediocre or something that blows people away?

Being prepared also means always showing up on time. When I was a young sales manager, I would lock the door to a meeting so people couldn't enter the room after the start time. If the meeting was at 8:00, the door was locked at 8:00. This trained people that showing up on time was non-negotiable. But on the flip side of that, because I was holding others accountable, I had to be prepared as well and lead a stellar meeting as soon as the clock hit 8:00.

In addition to the "micro" preparation of being prepared to do your job each day, you'll also want to think about the "macro" preparation of preparing for the next role you want to advance into.

Let's say a new model is being released by the manufacturer. It hasn't arrived yet, but there's information about it on the internet and in the news. You go into a sales meeting and the manager says, "By the way, we have a new model that should be out in a few months." What if you were able to say, "Oh, I've done some research on that. Here are the features of the car. Here's our main competition. Here are some ways I brainstormed how we can overcome the customer's objections to buying this car." You've done your homework, and you're ahead of the game.

When you're proactive in everything you do, it will be noticed. Then, when there's an opening for a new sales manager, for example, you'll be an obvious candidate because you've already taken the initiative to act like a sales manager.

It's key to carefully choose your moment to show that you're ready for the next role. In the wrong context, demonstrating that you're prepared can look like showing off or kissing up to your boss. The key is to make sure that the information you're sharing is relevant and helpful to others. If you take thirty minutes in a meeting to share information that isn't helpful to the team, you've just wasted others' time to show off what you know.

If you want to move up to the next role, spend some time talking to the person in that role and asking them questions. But you need to earn the right to sit next to this person... Don't waste their time. The way you earn that right is by coming to work on time, dressing well, participating in meetings, and being prepared with relevant questions to ask them. If you do all of these things, you'll begin to be recognized as someone the organization wants to keep long-term. When you ask for the opportunity to learn about another role, your superiors will listen because they're interested in seeing you move up, too. But if you don't do these things, when you ask about another role, your boss will think, "Are you kidding me? You don't even do the job you're in now."

CHAPTER 6

Commitment

The word "commitment" is thrown around all the time. What does it really mean to commit to something wholeheartedly, and why should you commit?

As I've matured, in my life and career, I'm careful about what I commit to, as I expect myself to go all in once I do commit to a goal or project. But I don't overanalyze things, either. If I commit myself to a change, I set goals, have daily plans, and monitor my progress. If I make a commitment to a project with others or with people I coach, I expect them to commit to the process as much as I commit to it.

This ensures that we will get as much success out of our projects and goals as possible. Commitment isn't just saying, "I'm in," it's saying, "I'm still in when things might not be going well or as planned." It's getting past the hurdles and roadblocks on growth and projects. This is the part of the journey where you learn to grow the most. This process is invaluable as your career grows, and you reflect on these times knowing that you have what it takes to get through it all.

When we're talking about commitment, you can't just say you're going to do something. You need to follow through and actually do it consistently. Commitment and self-discipline are intertwined. When you're committed to something, you're saying that you're going to make it happen no matter what. You have to understand that there's going to be problems, there's going to be roadblocks, and things are going to pop up. How you handle these things is a big part of your commitment. Do you let these roadblocks stop you? Or do you persevere and remain committed?

Your commitment affects how other people view you...

When we have a big project, and I ask for everyone's commitment and someone says yes but then they don't follow through...Why would I give this person the next project? People who aren't committed don't get opportunities because others view them as unreliable.

There's a video of Kobe Bryant talking about how he would watch how his teammates behaved in practice. Who showed up early? Who showed up late? Who was prepared and putting in effort to grow? Who was just coasting? Who was committed to winning, and who only said they were committed, but didn't act as though they were? He would think, "Why should I pass you the ball if you're not committed to helping the team win?" Everyone wants to get the ball and make a winning play when the cameras are on and there's an audience cheering, but not everyone is committed to showing up to practice ready to put in the work to make that possible.

It's the same in the workplace. Your teammates and bosses see what you do every day. If it seems like you aren't committed to the business based on your actions, why should they choose you when the next big opportunity or project comes along?

Commitment is not saying, "I'll sign up for the good stuff." It's saying, "I'll be there for the bad stuff, too." Commitment is not what you're capable of, it's what you are willing to do.

My wife likes to say every person has two sets of friends: the ones who only show up when you're throwing the barbecue, and the ones who show up when you're struggling and need help.

Many people want to accept the award without doing the work. But if you're truly committed, you'll be there even when the task ahead isn't fun or exciting.

Are you truly committed to being successful or are you just talking? Are you willing to put in the effort and deal with the pain of growth, the pain of failure, and the pain of discipline? Or do you just want to collect the award without putting in the work to earn it?

Are you all in? Are you prepared to stay committed even when you hit a roadblock?

While I was a General Manager of Mercedes-Benz of Fresno, the store was owned by Asbury Automotive Group at the time, and they were selling all of their dealerships in California. We were just coming out of the recession in 2010, and knowing they were selling the dealership, I had built a great relationship with our CEO and inquired about buying the dealership. They allowed me to pursue my dream of ownership, and I began my search for investment partners.

It's pretty hard to buy a Mercedes-Benz dealership when you only have $100,000 to your name. But I was committed to making it happen, so I drained my bank account and was able to secure financing. After several attempts with different partners, it finally happened in 2011, and we bought the dealership. I remember business was just starting to come back, and people would ask me what my "plan B" was if it did not work out. I would tell them, "I am fully committed to plan A, I don't want a Plan B." Having a Plan B means you are already looking for a safety net and are not truly committed to Plan A. So I went to work solely committed to my goal of ownership and continued overcoming many obstacles to see my vision of owning multiple stores and building a $100m company from that day forward play out. Your plan can change, but your goal should not. Don't settle for anything less than Plan A.

> "When I pull into the driveway at night, I'll look at myself in the rearview mirror and ask myself, 'Did you do every little possible thing that you could to be successful today?'"
>
> –Adam, my mentee

To commit to your personal growth goals, create a list of 5-10 "non-negotiables" that you do every day. These non-negotiables could look like: Do a 30-minute workout, drink 5 glasses of water, and read 20 pages of a sales strategy book so I can perform better at work.

These are the commitments you're making to yourself that will allow you to move toward your big-picture goals. Your non-negotiables can shift over time as your goals and priorities change, so it's a good idea to set a specific time to commit to them (such as 30 days) before pausing to reevaluate and setting new non-negotiables or renewing your current ones. If you can commit to your non-negotiables, over time, you'll see huge results.

CHAPTER 7

Avoiding Sabotage

When you set out on your growth journey, you may find that others, many of whom you may have previously called friends, try to sabotage you.

People who are insecure and afraid to begin their growth journeys may, consciously or unconsciously, try to keep you from growing and leaving them behind. This includes co-workers, friends, and even family members.

It can be tempting to succumb to this peer pressure. Let's say a salesperson, John, has begun his growth journey in the hopes of getting promoted next year. Before he began his growth journey, he and the other salespeople would go to a local bar after work to drink beer, watch sports, and complain about their boss.

John likes his coworkers, and he has fun with them, but he's now noticed that they have negative mindsets and never strive to improve themselves. He stops going out with them after work because one of his new goals is to wake up early and go to the gym. John's buddies notice this, and they try to pressure him to come. "Come on, John, lighten up and have some fun." John, not wanting to let his friends down, goes to the bar. He wakes up the next morning feeling sluggish, and due to his low energy, he fails to close a sale.

He resolves to not make the same mistake again. Then John notices his friends starting to make negative comments about his changing habits. They make jokes like, "Oh, he's too good for us now." How can John tune out these negative reactions to his growth so he can stay on track to get promoted next year?

John needs to surround himself with winners.

When you start to grow and win big, you won't have time to listen to negative people. You'll want to surround yourself with other winners. This doesn't mean you need to cut old friends out of your life completely, but seeking out new peers who share the same priorities as you will motivate you to stay on track.

When you start to put effort in, you will get pulled into bigger and better circles. You might be invited to dinners and high-caliber events... You might even get asked to speak or present at a conference or sales meeting. Each of these experiences widens your circle and fills it with driven, ambitious people who are committed to growth.

As you get promoted through the ranks, you'll be surrounded by "higher up" people who are all there because they have a winner's mindset. You become part of a more elite group. For example, if your organization awards you an opportunity to go to a retreat or conference, you'll build relationships with other successful people who go on this trip. Then, at the next meeting, you'll be sitting with this group. You'll gravitate towards each other because you spent time together and winners recognize winners.

If you're struggling to find successful people to connect with, I recommend using LinkedIn. If you see a sales manager at another organization posting that his organization won a national ranking, you can write him a message saying "Congrats on your success... Do you have a couple of minutes? I'd love to introduce myself to you and pick your brain on what you're doing in your store."

People often hold themselves back from sending these kinds of messages thinking, "These successful people get all kinds of requests like this. Why would they connect with me?" But most successful people don't get a lot of message requests because most people are afraid to send the message in the first place.

Personally, a younger competitor who's just getting started in his career recently reached out to me in this way. I was happy to say yes—though his organization is our competitor, there's so much opportunity out there that they won't put a dent in our business, and I want to "pay it forward" because other people did the same thing for me when I was early in my career.

I have many close friends who are car dealers. Even though we're selling against each other in the same city, we'll share advice and celebrate each other's successes. I tell people it's like playing golf. I can only concentrate and play my ball.

I can't play yours, so why would I worry about it? There's enough opportunity out there for all of us to be successful, so we might as well collaborate and share our wisdom. And even if I share what I know, they have to go and do the work to implement it themselves, so it's not as though any of us are "stealing" success from each other.

Relationships with other successful people are hugely valuable because they get you thinking on a different plane.

When you spend time with people who are at a level above you, they're thinking about totally different things than you are now...Conversely, you can be a mentor to those a level below you and open their eyes to how you think.

When you're surrounded by other successful people, it's easy to drown out the negative voices standing in your way.

And the longer you execute your habits, the easier it becomes to stay on track...

When your pilot light gets lit and your momentum of growth starts to burn inside you to become your best self personally and professionally, that fire becomes so hot that you won't want to miss a workout, you won't want to miss a meeting at work, you won't want to miss a monthly goal. You'll become so focused that the opportunity to be sabotaged becomes less and less. You will be so busy crushing work and life that you simply will not have time for it.

Your willpower becomes stronger than peer pressure. Once you start to win and get to that level, it will give you the power to tell people, "Go away, I'm on a roll. I'm done messing around."

Still, occasionally the negative voices can get through. In these moments of doubt, when people in your life are acting as roadblocks to your success, ask yourself, "What's more important to me, achieving my dreams and goals or letting other influences throw me off course?"

What happens when you get off course?

Nobody's perfect. At some point, we'll all mess up and get off track with our goals. If this happens, what do we do?

If you miss one day, get back on track the next day.

If you miss two days, you MUST get back on track the next day.

If you miss three days, your body and mind go back to comfort. The fire inside is now starting to go down from a blaze back to a pilot light. The red alert should be going off. Get back on track NOW.

If you miss a week or more, you're starting over.

For example, you have a goal to work out every morning... What happens if you miss one day? You go to work lacking energy, so you don't make much progress toward your professional goals. The next day, get up and work out so you're back on track.

Don't beat yourself up for missing a day—instead, take action to get back on track.

If you miss a week or more, you have to start over. You may still have muscle memory there, so if you engage back in the process quickly, you might be able to get back on track. It's crucial to begin again with full commitment because your mind and body are starting to say, "I'm awfully comfortable not doing this stuff." Review your journal of your growth and progress to remember your wins and why you were committed in the first place. This is why journaling is important...if you fall off the wagon with your exercise routine and never document your successes, you might think, "Oh, well, I give up." But if you have a record of all the days you successfully worked out with notes that say, "Worked out today. Felt great and gave me the energy to prepare for the presentation," you'll feel motivated to get back on track.

When I say "miss a week," I'm not talking about taking a week-long vacation. Sometimes, you've earned a vacation, and you may not want to wake up at 5 a.m. and journal when you're in a beach house with your family. But if you've committed to physical workouts for a long enough amount of time, you may find that you'll want to keep up your workout routine while on vacation because you'll feel the difference in your body and mind without it. But maybe that shifts from a 5 a.m. intense gym workout to a walk through nature with your family.

You may even find you don't want to go without journaling for a week. I used to vacation in Kauai in January and stay in a house that was right on the water. I would wake up early to have a quiet moment alone to journal, read my motivational book, and outline my goals for the year.

If you do take time off of your routines on vacation then launch right into them the first day back home—don't get comfortable missing them. I will say that most of the elite business people on the top of their game do not take days off of continuous growth, even on vacation. They push themselves physically with a good early workout, read a good book or two, and plan their next big goal and where the next vacation will be when they hit that goal. Again, they want that furnace burning as hot as ever when they get back from "vacation".

Growth is a lifelong process. It's likely that, at some point, you'll get off track. As long as you know how to get back on track and recommit to your goals, one failure won't be the end of the world.

CHAPTER 8

The Importance of a Mentor

To continue to be successful, it's helpful to have a mentor—someone with more wisdom and experience in a certain area who can guide you on your journey to accomplishing your goals.

How do you find a mentor? It tends to happen naturally. You meet someone professionally or socially who has expertise in an area that you want to have expertise in and make a connection. You feel they would be open to sharing their experiences, so you ask them to get lunch or coffee. From there, the relationship develops naturally. After a while, you'll find yourself introducing this person as your friend and mentor.

It works the same way with a mentee... It starts with seeing someone who is putting in the work to grow and recognizing that sharing some of the lessons I've learned could help them. I'll invite them to chat, I'll share any knowledge I have that could help them with their goals, and the relationship builds from there.

A good mentor:

- Is a truth teller...A mentor should be honest with you and not sugarcoat things you could improve on.
- Is a good listener...Sometimes, you just need someone to listen to you talk through your ideas or roadblocks and let you come to your conclusions.
- Always answer your call—because they know you're committed to growth.
- Gets joy from watching you win—as much as, if not more than they like winning themselves.

A good mentee:

- Is committed to growth
- Is motivated and "has the pilot light on"
- Is a goal setter...has a vision for where they want to go
- Listens
- Takes action on your input
- Emulates you but puts their own unique spin on your advice...Success is not just about copying and pasting what someone else has done...Your mentee should innovate on your advice and come up with an even better solution

Your mentor can be younger than you in age...Mentorship is about experience. My spiritual mentor is a younger buddy of mine who's a pastor. He may be younger than me, but he has more experience and expertise in thinking about spirituality.

"I would not be where I am today without a mentor. I've had multiple mentors throughout my career, and every mentor relationship is built on respect. It's like an unspoken agreement where the mentor looks at you and says, "Hey, you have something that is pretty special, and I'm going to help you get to the next spot because I believe in you." I wouldn't be where I am today without my mentors, but I also had to pull my own weight.

When you have a mentor who believes in you, you're happy to show up to work and go the extra mile. You always want to make your mentor proud. You want to take the ball from your mentor and run it all the way to the finish line.

> A good mentor can empower you to grow and become a leader. When I worked with Scott, I would often go to him and ask, "What do you want me to do?" He would reply, "You know what to do." This taught me that I had the autonomy to make decisions—and I even had the autonomy to make mistakes."
>
> –Spencer, my mentee

Building Your Mentor Team

You don't have to stop at one mentor... Ideally, you'll build a team of mentors that encompasses each area of your life where you want to grow:

- Physical health
- Mental health
- Spiritual health
- Financial health

You can't have the financial health without the other 3:

You need to get your physical health in order so you have the energy and stamina to succeed at work.

You need to get your mental health in order so you can handle stress and have clarity about your goals.

And you need to get your spiritual health in order so you can connect your life to a higher purpose and find meaning.

Once you get those three things, it's easier to find financial health and be successful in your career—it tends to take care of itself. But if you chase financial health first and ignore the other three, you'll have nothing.

One of the great values of having a mentor or coach is just having someone watching what you're doing—even that passive level of accountability is going to make you do better. It's like the old adage: "What gets measured improves." Even better, what is measured and then shared with others is even more likely to improve. For example, I have a virtual personal trainer who lives in LA and texts and calls me to hold me accountable for my diet and fitness goals. If I'm tempted to break one of my habits, the thought of having to confess to her that I messed up motivates me to stay on track.

Even if the person in each area isn't a mentor you form a deep relationship with, at the very least find a trusted guide who checks in with you weekly in each area and holds you accountable to your goals as an "outside eye."

Why Mentoring Others is a Key to Advancement

Most people want to be mentored, yet the best way to move up and be mentored yourself is to mentor others. Here's how to think about it: If you want to get promoted, have your replacement trained. Train and mentor your replacement for the role you're in now.

Hiring smart, dedicated, motivated people for a position is difficult. If I promote you, how do I replace you? Having your replacement trained shows leadership skills, commitment to the organization, and your ability to assess the needs of the company, which makes you a huge asset.

A salesperson, Joe, sells twenty cars a month. The salesman below that is Mark, who sells twelve cars a month. The finance manager position at the organization opens up. If I promote Joe, I'm losing twenty sales a month and profits are going to go down. But if Joe mentors Mark and teaches him how to sell twenty cars a month, I know I can promote Joe without losing our organization's strongest salesperson and lowering our profits.

If you don't mentor someone to take your place, the boss may look outside the organization for someone to hire rather than promoting you so they won't lose a successful person in your role.

Yet, if you're able to go to the boss and say, "I really want to be the finance manager. I know you think you're going to lose twenty car sales a month if I get moved to finance, but let me show you why you're not. Not only am I going to move to finance, I'm going to help train your salespeople. While I'm doing my finance job, I want to be involved in new hire training and mentor the current salespeople. I want to teach them how I've been successful in the role," it'll be a no-brainer for the boss to promote you to finance because you've positioned yourself as a leader.

Mentoring others is a gift. You can give back to others what people have given to you. It gives me satisfaction watching others grow to their full potential—sometimes it makes me as happy as if they were my own children.

My favorite part of owning and running successful organizations was coaching and mentoring others. I wrote this book to share my knowledge and success with others so I can be a mentor on a bigger scale.

CHAPTER 9

Do you have a coaching organization?

If you don't coach your employees, someone else will... When employees aren't being pushed to grow by their organizations, they may (and should) seek coaching outside of the organization.

With the organizations I've been a part of, my experience is that nearly all have processes in place that train employees on sales, customer service, and customer retention.

Yet, when it comes to the people side, coaching up the staff for business and personal growth, and preparing current and future leaders to grow into bigger roles, they do not have the internal trainers, curriculum, and programs to move the needle.

The companies that prioritize personal and professional growth within their culture tend to have lower turnover and a greater ability to promote leaders from within because they are developing leadership bench strength. It is a natural byproduct of the focus on personal and professional growth.

"There's a difference between management and leadership. A manager or boss can tell you what you're doing wrong, but that might not fix anything. When you have true leadership in an organization, you can feel it. A leader pushes everyone to grow."

–Spencer, my mentee

Happier, more successful employees turn into higher profits and more sales for the organization. Instead of having to recruit, people are lined up ready to join that organization based on current employee feedback and reputation. Instead of having to say, "I need to go out and hire," people are lined up at your door to come to work for you because they know if they do, they're going to have personal growth, professional growth, and a better life.

When that happens, your organization goes through the roof because you're getting the best of the best all of the time. When a position opens up in your company, your employees are calling their friends at other organizations saying, "Hey, I know you've been in your current job for five years and you feel stuck in a rut. Come here, and you'll be able to grow."

Personal growth is a huge bonus that doesn't show up on the paycheck.

When you weave personal growth into the culture of your organization, everyone, from the top to the bottom, becomes a leader.

You as the owner are now THE leader coaching a team of leaders. The leader at the top sets the focus and standard, raises up leaders under that, and coaches them. The culture of leadership moves down through the organization.

When I was running a Mercedes-Benz dealership, my dealership won an award for the best Mercedes-Benz dealership to work for based on employee surveys. Before we got that award, we were having a luncheon, and the employees surprised my wife and me by giving us a huge, beautiful award that said, "Scott and Katie Biehl, The Best Leaders. Thank you for your continued efforts in making Mercedes-Benz such a special place to work, from your employees and extended family." They had all chipped in and bought us an award with their own money.

This award didn't come out of nowhere. We had earned it by proving to our team that we were committed to helping all of them grow to their full potential and achieve success.

We led by example, demonstrating the principles of personal growth that are now documented in this book, and we influenced everyone in our organization to begin their growth journey.

When I noticed people were striving for growth, I would bring them into my office and talk to them about their goals, no matter where they were on the totem pole of employees. I would invite them to things outside of work that aligned with their goals and watch as they became more and more invested in improving themselves as I led by example.

At one point, I was into rowing before work, and I had a few employees decide to join me in this routine. Other employees would meet up with me to go running in the park. People would come to a Bible study I told them I was going to. I influenced others to grow simply by committing to my own growth and showing them how it led to success.

It even spread beyond our employees to their families: My wife was a running coach and ran half marathons, so some employees' wives decided to join her coaching program and start running.

Growth starts at the top.

Coaching is about elevating everyone in your organization into being a leader, whether they're in a position of leadership or not. When a growth mindset spreads throughout your organization, employees are empowered to achieve personal and professional goals, and the organization enjoys greater profits and customer satisfaction.

> "When I first started working with Scott, he told me to park in the back corner of the lot and walk in to work the long way—through the whole service department, the whole parts department, and the whole office—and pick one person each day to introduce myself to on that morning walk. I made a point of doing that and having real, human conversations with each person in the organization–and seeking out those who were looking for personal growth."
>
> –Adam, my mentee

The Right Meetings

Organizations tend to be good at training processes and sales techniques...all those things that they believe will lead to a sale or better customer service. But what they don't have down is coaching...Coaching develops the person into a better employee and a better person. Coaching gives employees the feeling that they're part of a bigger picture and not just showing up to collect a paycheck.

Coaching can inspire people and introduce them to fresh ideas for improving themselves, which ends up bettering the organization.

But coaching doesn't mean more generic team meetings that lead nowhere. Coaching is about implementing the right meetings that the team needs based on intuitively observing where there's an opportunity for growth. Do I need to pull a particular person in for a one-on-one? Do I need to lead by example on a certain topic? Do I need to pull the team together and reinforce the bigger vision in a group setting?

To coach effectively, I recommend having a one-on-one meeting with the 5-10 people who directly report to you at least once a month. You can have sidebar meetings as questions, problems, or opportunities come up, but at least consistently have a monthly check-in.

During this meeting, cover:

- What are the goals that month for the individual?
- What is their plan to achieve those goals?
- How will they track progress toward this goal?

These meetings address professional goals, but I like to also ask the employee what their personal goal is for the month to reinforce the idea that personal and professional growth are connected.

Have that plan in writing so then throughout the month, you can follow up with the individual and track their progress. If things are going well, you can encourage them, and if they're falling behind, it's the coach's responsibility to pull the person aside and hold them accountable to get back on track. "You said you were going to make 20 calls a day. Are you doing that?"

It's also important in these meetings to probe the employee's plan to ensure it will work.

If a car manager came to me and said, "Hey boss, we're going to sell 100 new cars this month," instead of me saying, "Okay, 100 new cars, got it," and letting him go, I would say, "I want to know how you're going to get to that 100." I'd listen to him list out the types. Then, I would pull up the inventory and say, "Well, you say you're going to sell five S classes, but we only have one in stock. Do we have more coming in?" "Well, no." "Then why did you write five down?" This questioning ensures that the employee builds an action plan that will get the goal accomplished.

You can't just write down a goal and listen to everyone cheer. You have to inspect the plan and make sure it can work.

Knowing Vs Doing Problems

When an employee makes a mistake, ask yourself if it's a knowing problem or a doing problem.

Did the employee have the information and training needed to do their job? If not, it's your responsibility to give this employee the knowledge they need to succeed.

If the employee had the knowledge but simply didn't execute the task in the right way, it's a "doing" problem, which usually reflects on the employee. Making this distinction makes it easier to identify a solution when something is going wrong, rather than blaming an employee who may not have had the correct information and/or training.

It's important to note that not every employee will "drink the Kool-Aid" about personal growth—and that's okay. I still had good employees in the organization who didn't want to be coached. I need them as employees, but when it came to promotions, those who were on board with personal growth were much better suited to move up than those who were not. Those employees were "Driven to Succeed."

Sometimes, employees who aren't buying into growth may just take longer to come to the party. As they watch others grow and succeed, they may change their minds and get caught up in the momentum created by others.

Some of your employees may have had previous bosses who were "all talk and no action" when it came to growth. This can make employees skeptical of this initiative. It's imperative to be consistent in your coaching to show your employees that you're serious about transforming the organization.

Though not everyone will find it easy to commit to growth, you need enough of your key people to have this drive to be able to create a world-class organization.

CHAPTER 10

The Payoff

Once you set out on the growth path, there is no destination…

The journey never ends.

You don't suddenly stop striving for growth once you hit your goal. With each goal you hit, the bar keeps rising, and you'll pursue more ambitious goals that bring you more success and fulfillment.

To sustain the growth, fall in love with the process of it, not the result.

The fun part is that at some point, your growth will start to pay off. Finally, the rewards for all of the tedious, boring day-to-day work you put in over the years will come to you. But I think you'll find that the biggest reward is how you feel inside. You've learned to master your mind and you've gained control over your destiny, which is something most people never do in life.

Once you start growing, you won't want to stop... You'll think, "How much better can I get? How high can I go?"

You'll find that you keep raising the bar for your expectations.

Most high achievers will tell you that before they've even reached a goal, they already have a higher goal in mind for when they reach their current goal and hit a plateau. Visually, they've already hit their current goal. If a general sales manager wants to be a general manager and is working towards that goal, he's already visualizing himself as the general manager... So in the back of his mind, he's already set the next goal to be a dealer.

I'm still not done. I worked my way up through the ranks, starting my career as a 21-year-old car salesperson with a high school diploma and became a dealer, owned multiple stores, became a CEO, built a $100m plus organization, and sold the company. But my journey still isn't over... I wanted to challenge myself to grow further, so I decided to turn my focus to teaching others how to grow. This book exists because I asked myself, "What's my next goal? How can I keep winning and getting better?" Writing a book was another way to step out of my comfort zone and push myself to achieve something I'd never done before.

When you master what is in this book, you can teach what you've learned to others.

The return on teaching is infinite. When you teach someone, they teach others, and those people teach others, and it goes on and on. Your impact becomes exponential.

Teaching makes you a leader, and when you're viewed as a leader, you'll be able to rise to higher and higher positions in your organization and the industry.

> "If you take quitting off the table, what options do you have left? In a sales meeting, I once asked my staff that question. I got each person to tell me everything they could do that wasn't quitting. At the end of the meeting, I told them, 'Guess what? No one quit, so let's go.'"
>
> –Spencer, my mentee

Discipline = Freedom

Discipline equals freedom, both in your personal and professional life. I hate to see people in their personal lives get so out of whack on something that they can't enjoy what they once had the freedom to do. A perfect example of this is when someone goes from being overweight to obese and now has other physical issues to contend with. The doctor advises that person to go on a strict diet to avoid health complications. This person loved having friends and family over for pizza, but now they can't eat it. They have had their freedom of choice taken away due to their own lack of discipline about health. Most likely, had they initiated daily healthy habits they could have avoided this situation and still have the freedom to eat what they want at certain times. Discipline equals freedom.

On the professional side, the discipline you put in at work makes you productive while you are there. When you're more productive and able to finish your work in less time, you have more time available to spend doing things you enjoy or with family and friends.

I'd like to tell you that implementing all the things from this book will lead you to success and that it becomes easier—and that you will not have to continue to do the discipline, habits, and actions to stay ahead. But remember, your competition is also trying to get better and grow as individuals and as an organization.

Teams that win in pro sports are back to work days after winning an NBA final, a Super Bowl, or a World Series. The same goes for the MVP, the individual. This is also true when you're at the top. After a team has a big win, you might see a picture of the owner smiling and holding up the trophy. But two days later, the owner is in panic mode, back to work again: "What players are retiring? How are we going to draft new players? Is our coaching staff going to get poached?" No success is final, even if you're the world champion. It takes discipline to stay at the top once you reach it.

When you become number one, your competitors think, "Wait a minute…I don't like being number two. What can I do to win?" You've set their next target for them… So rather than sitting back and celebrating your success, how do you raise the bar so you can stay on top?

How many times have you seen a golf tournament where they said, "Last year, the winner of this tournament shot 17 under. This year, the winner shot 23 under" and there were five people this year who shot 17 under, beating last year's winner, and still lost the tournament?

Once a bar is set, everyone's goal is to hit that bar. If you're the one who set the bar, you'll have to keep raising the bar higher and higher unless you want your competitors to catch up to you.

On this journey, you'll find that consistency gets boring. That's why it's crucial to always have a clear goal in mind. Without a goal, consistency gets so monotonous that you quit. But when you have a goal, you know that all the boring, difficult tasks you're undertaking each day will eventually lead you to your dreams. If you're running a race, no matter how bored you are when you're pounding the pavement, you keep going because you know every step is a step closer to the finish line.

You don't get to the top without the boredom of consistency. Without some agony over losses, you will never experience the joy of your wins. Once you commit to your goals, you need to embrace the reality that will take everything you have to achieve them. Embrace that journey. You will never regret it.

When you become successful, appreciate all the amazing things you've accomplished... Once you've done that, get back to work!

CONCLUSION

Now that you know what the path to personal growth looks like, what are you waiting for?

It's time to take the first step and apply the principles we've explored in this book.

Take some time to write down your big-picture goals and the non-negotiable habits you can implement to get there. (The 30-Day Challenge is a great place to start.) When you wake up tomorrow, you're off! Complete your non-negotiables and notice how doing so elevates your confidence and energy. Each day, notice the difference in how you feel physically and mentally and how others perceive you.

After days, weeks, months, and years of commitment to personal growth, you'll observe the full effects of your transformation. You'll be elevated to a position you thought would take years to reach.

Your boss will look to you when there are new opportunities to demonstrate your abilities.

You'll impress everyone at your organization as you excel in your role, and your peers will look at you with a new respect.

When you walk into a room, everyone from co-workers to clients will feel that you're a confident, capable leader.

In your personal life, your family and friends will gain a new admiration for you as they watch you push toward a better future, and you may find yourself attracting new friends into your social circle who are drawn to your high-achieving mindset. Due to your energy, purpose, and drive, you'll wake up each morning excited to challenge yourself and take on whatever the day brings.

Best of all, you'll always have the knowledge that you can achieve anything you want to through self-discipline and perseverance. Once you unlock the ability to live in this way, no one can take that from you. You'll be unstoppable.

But it would be all too easy to put down this book without taking action and return to the status quo. The sooner you take action, the likelier it is that you'll successfully launch your personal growth journey. Don't let fear pull you back into your comfort zone…

Push forward and become the person you've always wanted to be.

If you're ready to begin your personal growth journey and want a guide with decades of experience in the automotive industry, reach out to me (scott@driventosucceed.coach). I work with a small number of ambitious, driven people who want to succeed beyond their wildest dreams.

BONUS CHAPTER

The 30 Day Challenge

If you're ready to begin implementing the principles in this book, I've created a 30-day challenge to jumpstart your growth.

Can you commit to this morning routine for 30 days in a row?

The first hour of the day, follow these 10 "non-negotiables":

- Put your phone in airplane mode.
- Pray about or reflect on what you're grateful for.
- Drink 16oz of water.
- Drink your morning coffee–no sugar.
- Review today's task list & visualize success.
- Perform physical activity to warm up your brain and body. (Ex: walk, run, row, cycle, yoga, pilates, strength train)
- If you listen to anything, choose uplifting music or a positive podcast.
- Don't make any excuses to interrupt this hour…The next 23 hours you can deal with the world, but this hour is for you. You've earned it.

- You can't use your hour to sleep in, you must move your body and wake up your mind.
- Repeat every day, including workdays, days off, and holidays. Never stop.

SCAN ME

Download your own checklist at driventosucceed.coach.

If you can follow these ten rules every morning for 30 days straight, snap a photo and post it to social media with the hashtag #driventosucceed to join our Winner's Circle.

If you fail to do any of these things, your 30 days start over. There are no excuses. If you skip this routine one Sunday because you want to watch football instead, you don't get to post that you completed the challenge. If this happens, don't beat yourself up, but start over the next day.

The purpose of the 30-day challenge is to cultivate self-discipline. Doing these for 30 days establishes them as a habit and teaches you how to commit to building new habits for a month. After you've completed the challenge, it'll be easier for you to set new monthly goals and stick to them for 30 days.

These are easy things to do...and the problem is that they are easy not to do. Though each of the ten steps may be easy to complete, the difficulty comes in consistently executing them every day, no matter what. There will be mornings when you think, "It's so nice and warm under my blanket...What if I slept in for thirty minutes?" Or "It's so cold outside this morning...Do I really have to go for a run?". These moments are where the true challenge of this morning routine lies. Do you have the discipline and determination to push past these excuses and stick to your routine even when it's easier not to? This morning routine trains your mind to be consistent.

Starting your mornings with a distraction-free hour to get your mind and body ready for the day is powerful. The things on the list are things that are going to take you to the goal you're trying to achieve. If you don't do these things, you'll fall further and further behind on your goal. You'll get frustrated because you're not getting promoted, moving up in your career, or making more money.

When you do these things, all the other things you have to do during the day that you thought were going to be really hard suddenly become not that big of a deal because you'll already have a feeling of accomplishment at the beginning of your day.

Note that I haven't even told you what time to wake up— this routine is just for the first hour of the day. You don't have to be a member of the "4 a.m. club" if this doesn't fit your work schedule. If you're a salesperson who works from 2 p.m. until midnight, you may not get up and execute your morning routine until 9 a.m. Meanwhile, someone whose shift starts early in the morning might wake up at 5 a.m. to start the routine. Choose whichever start time works for you… What matters is consistently devoting the first hour of your day to these tasks.

Are you ready to commit to the challenge? Start tomorrow morning, and I hope to hear about your success in 30 days. In fact, email me at scott@driventosucceed.coach and tell me in a few sentences why YOU are "Driven to Succeed" and that you are starting on the first 30 days of your commitment journey.

ABOUT THE AUTHOR

Scott Biehl resides in beautiful Lake Tahoe with his wife of 30 years. Scott spent the last 35 years in the retail automotive business rising from a 21-year-old salesperson to becoming the Owner, CEO, and Dealer Principal of the #1 Jaguar Land Rover dealership in the USA. Although Scott sold his dealerships in 2022 he is far from retired. Scott's passion has always focused on helping others succeed. Scott has a successful consulting and coaching business for both individuals and organizations through the Driven to Succeed network where he not only coaches and consults but also delivers multi-day training events. Scott can be reached by email at scott@driventosucceed.coach. To find out more about the Driven to Succeed program, upcoming events, merchandise or to contact Scott about a speaking engagement at your next event please visit Scott's website at DriventoSucceed.coach

THE CAREER OF SCOTT BIEHL:
PEDAL TO THE METAL FOR FOUR DECADES

1987: OUT OF THE KITCHEN. ONTO THE SALES FLOOR.

At 21, Scott leaves his job as a short order cook to sell cars at a Mitsubishi dealership. With only $300 to his name and a high school diploma, he buys two white shirts, one tie and a pair of slacks and sells 15 cars in just 12 days. Two months later, he buys his first house.

1991: FROM SALESMAN TO FINANCE MANAGER.

Scott is hired as a Finance Manager to open a new dealership, Honda North in Clovis, CA

1993: NEXT STOP: SALES MANAGER

Scott earns promotion to Sales Manager at Honda North, driving them to become the #1 selling Honda dealership in the market for 10 straight years.

2003: SLIPPING INTO SOMETHING MORE LUXURIOUS

Scott is hired by Asbury Automotive Group to become the General Sales Manager of Mercedes-Benz of Fresno.

2004: QUICK PROMOTION AND KEY AWARD

In just 6 short months, Scott is promoted to General Manager of Mecedes-Benz of Fresno and wins his first of many coveted "Best of the Best" award from Mercedes-Benz USA.

2009: STEPPING INTO THE SPOTLIGHT

Scott is selected as the keynote speaker at Asbury Annual Executive meeting in Orlando, FL -delivering his speech in front of 125 of his peers as well as the Executive Board of publicly traded Asbury Automotive Group (NYSE: ABG)

2011: SCOTT LIKES THE DEALERSHIP SO MUCH, HE BUYS IT!

Scott puts a partnership group together and buys his dealership Mercedes-Benz of Fresno with automotive icons Ray Beshoff and Jerry Heuer as his partners.

2015: ACCOLADES CONTINUE ROLLING IN.
Scott is awarded "Best Dealership to Work For" by MBUSA and also receives his 10th consecutive "Best Luxury Auto Dealership in Fresno" Award.

2019: ANOTHER PARTNERSHIP. ANOTHER POWER MOVE.
Scott puts together his second partnership group with Mike McKee (former CEO of the Irvine Company and current Chairman of the Tiger Woods Foundation, TGR) and together they buy out Beshoff and Heuer, forming Triunity Automotive Group with Scott serving as Dealer Principal and CEO.

2021: MAKING HIS MARK IN ANOTHER JUNGLE.
Triunity purchases Hornburg Jaguar Land Rover in West Hollywood and Scott builds a 100,000 square foot state of the art facility, changes the name to Jaguar Land Rover Los Angeles and making it the #1 Jaguar and Land Rover dealer in the USA.

2022: THE END OF THE ROAD IS THE BEGINNING OF ANOTHER.
After building a $100 million dollar plus enterprise, Scott makes a strategic decision to sell the dealerships. But instead of riding off into the sunset, he launches his new coaching and consulting company in Incline Village, NV – Lake Tahoe.

2024: SHIFTING INTO A NEW GEAR
Scott Authors his first book, *Driven to Succeed* and opens a new office and executive training facility where he conducts multiple day coaching events in Incline Village where he resides full time now in beautiful Lake Tahoe. Scott is a sought-after speaker, coach and consultant, and host of the *Driven to Succeed* podcast.